Robots

KINGFISHER

a Houghton Mifflin Company imprint
222 Berkeley Street
Boston, Massachusetts 02116
www.houghtonmifflinbooks.com

First published in 2003
2 4 6 8 10 9 7 5 3 1

1TR/0503/PROSP/RNB(RNB)/140MA

LIBRARY OF CONGRESS CATALOGING-IN-PUBLICATION DATA
has been applied for.

ISBN 0-7534-5618-4

Senior editor: Belinda Weber
Coordinating editor: Stephanie Pliakas
Designer: Peter Clayman
Picture manager: Cee Weston-Baker
Picture researcher: Rachael Swann
DTP coordinator: Sarah Pfitzner
DTP operator: Primrose Burton
Artwork archivists: Wendy Allison, Jenny Lord
Senior production controller: Nancy Roberts
Indexer: Chris Bernstein

Printed in China

Acknowledgments
The Publisher would like to thank the following for permission to reproduce their material. Every care has been taken
to trace copyright holders. However, if there have been unintentional omissions or failure to trace copyright holders,
we apologize and will, if informed, endeavor to make corrections in any future edition.
b = bottom, c = center, l = left, t = top, r = right

Photographs: *cover*: Oscar Williams © 1997/ BBH Exhibits Inc. 6-7 *c* Sony/SDR-4X; 8-9 *l* Getty Images; *c* eMuu, Dr. Christoph Bartneck,
Technical University of Eindhoven; *br* Peter Menzel/Science Photo Library; 10-11 *bl* James King-Holmes/Science Photo Library; *br* Photo:
(Ingrid Friedl) Lufthansa Technik Skywash/Lufthansa, Putzmeister AG; *tr* Space and Naval Warfare Systems Center, San Diego;
12-13 *cl* © Randy Montoya, Sandia National Laboratories; *c* Robosaurus/Doug Malewicki, Monster Robot Inc., *tr* Coneyl Jay/Science Photo
Library; 14-15 *bl* Honda Asimo; *tr* Eriko Fugita/Reuters/Popperfoto; *c* Sam Ogden/Science Photo Library;16-17 *bl* Sony/AIBO ERS-220;
tr © Dr. Gavin Miller SnakeRobots.com, Copyright 2000; *r* BBH Exhibits Inc./Oscar Williams; 18-19 *cl* Richard Bachmann, Gabriel Nelson
and Roger Quinn at Case Western Reserve University; *bc* MIT, Bruce Frisch/Science Photo Library; *tr* Sarcos; 20-21 *tr* PA photos/Sony;
br PA photos; *tr, bl* TM Robotics (Europe) Ltd/Toshiba; 22-23 *bc* Associated Press; *bl* MIT Media Lab, Getty Images; *tr* NASA/Carnegie
Mellon University, Science Photo Library; 24-25 *bl* modelluboot@t-online.de (Norbert Brüggen); *c* Getty Images; *tr* Associated Press;
26-27 *bl* NASA/Science Photo Library; *tr* NASA/Science Photo Library; *br* Media Resource Center NASA/ Lyndon B. Johnson Space Center;
28-29 *tr* Courtesy of the School of Mechanical Engineering, The University of Western Australia; *b* Louisiana State University;
cr © Ron Sanford/CORBIS; *tl* Digital Vision; 30-31 *tc* PaPeRo/© NEC Corporation 2001-2003; *cl* © Roger Ressmeyer/Corbis; *br* Electric
handout/Reuters/Popperfoto; 32-33 *bl* Spencer Grant/Science Photo Library; *br* Roy Garner/Rex Features; *tr* CRASAR™/www.crasar.org;
34-35 *bl* Associated Press; *c* © Cynthia's Bar and Restaurant; *tr* Associated Press; 36-37 *bc* Peter Menzel/Science Photo Library;
cl r. AeroVironment Inc.; *tr* www.edwards.af/Edwards Air Force Base; 38-39 Peter Menzel/Science Photo Library;
40-41 *bl* Tri-Star for *Short Circuit*/Kobal; *bl* Sautelet, Jerrican /Science Photo Library; *tr* AAR Productions/Kobal.
Short Circuit Tri-Star Pictures; *Return of the Jedi* Lucasfilm; *Doctor Who* BBC TV

Commissioned photography on pages 42–47 by Andy Crawford.
Thank you to models Eleanor Davis, Lewis Manu, Daniel Newton, Lucy Newton, Nikolas Omilana, and Olivia Omilana.

Kingfisher Young Knowledge

Robots

Clive Gifford

KINGFISHER
BOSTON

Contents

What is a robot?

Robots are amazing machines that can work on their own. They can be used in many places—from space to deep underwater.

Eyes, ears, and mouth

Robots collect information about the world using devices called sensors. This Sony robot has sensors that record sound and cameras that take pictures.

sensors—*devices that give a robot information about its surroundings*

Handy workers

Robots can often do more than one task. Gripping hands allow them to hold and use many different tools and objects.

On the move

Many robots can move using wheels, tank tracks, or legs. This robot has knee and hip joints that work just like human legs.

8 Robot controllers

Controllers are a robot's brain. They make decisions for the robot and operate all of its parts. Robot controllers are usually computers.

Fast thinkers

Computers make decisions very quickly. *Deep Junior* can think through three million chess moves each second. Here it is playing the former World Chess champion, Garry Kasparov.

Showing emotion

This robot is called *eMuu*. It interacts with people and can show many different expressions, including happiness, anger, and sadness.

Learning to walk

Some robots are controlled directly by people. Others are able to work by themselves. This autonomous robot from Japan is teaching itself how to walk.

autonomous—able to work by itself

Robot arms

Robot arms are the most popular type of robot. They have joints, so the arm can move in many different directions—just like a human arm.

Get a grip!

Many robot arms end with a robot hand—called a gripper. Grippers are often made with pressure sensors to help them judge how much force is needed to grip something.

Robot guards

This robot security guard tracks down intruders. Its left arm carries a range finder. Its right arm controls a gun that can fire darts.

Jet wash

Skywash, a giant robot arm, cleans jumbo jets in record time. It takes about three hours to wash an airplane. Without the robot, it could take up to 12 hours.

Robots big and small

Robots come in many shapes and sizes. The largest are several feet high and weigh thousands of pounds. Different sized robots use different power systems to move their parts.

Mighty monster

Robosaurus is a huge car-crushing monster. It uses hydraulic power to lift and destroy cars, trucks, and even airplanes!

Marvelous *MARV*

MARV is a moving robot that is so small it can sit on a coin! Its tiny electric motor is powered by watch batteries. *MARV* can only move at a speed of 20 inches per minute.

hydraulic power—a power system using liquids to generate force

Shrinking small

One day robots may become so small that they will be able to travel inside our bodies! Robots might travel through our veins, cleaning and repairing them.

Humanoid robots

People are fascinated by machines that look and act just like them. Scientists are building humanoid robots that can carry out a wide range of skills.

Stair walkers

Scientists have figured out how to keep a two-legged robot upright when it walks. Honda's *ASIMO* robot can even climb stairs with ease.

Want a ride?

This humanoid robot from Asia acts like a ricksha driver, pulling people around. It is powered by motors in its head and chest.

Show your feelings

Kismet is one of the few robots that is able to show facial expressions. Its mouth, eyelids, eyebrows, and eyes all move to show expressions such as fear, happiness, disgust, interest, and surprise.

humanoid—*looking or acting like a person*

Robot animals

Some robots look like animals. This may be to make a museum exhibition more fun or to make animatronic models for movies. Scientists also borrow ideas from animals to make robots move smoothly.

Snakes alive

Snakes move by sliding their bodies across the ground. This robot *S5* snake can slide through pipes and other cramped spaces.

A new best friend

Sony's *AIBO ERS-220* is a new mobile robot that has been programmed to behave like a dog. It recognizes 75 different words and will respond to its owner calling its name.

animatronic—a model that uses computers and robotics to bring it to life

Standing tall

This robot giraffe uses
parts of machines to
show how the parts
of real animals work.
It looks down on
visitors at the Robot
Zoo exhibition on
its world tours.

Robot **insects**

Insects are very hardy creatures
that can live in many different places.
Robot makers have copied some insects
to help them build robots that can
work in extreme conditions.

Robo-roach!

Ajax is designed to look like a cockroach.
Its front legs each have five joints, and
the robot can stay balanced on just
three of its six legs.

Flying insects

This model of a monarch butterfly flaps its wings using muscle wires. These wires shorten in length when electricity is applied.

Creepy crawler!

Genghis was one of the first insect robots to be built. Its six legs allow it to move over bumpy ground. When it comes across something too big to climb over, *Genghis* simply backs off and chooses another route.

Having fun

Playing sports is a lot of fun for people, but for robots it is a test of their abilities. Robots need to be able to make quick decisions and move their parts rapidly to play sports.

Playing volleyball

These Japanese test robots are learning to play volleyball. Each robot uses cameras to track the path of the ball, timing the movement of its joints to meet the ball in midair.

Goal!

Balancing on one foot, this *Sony SDR-3X* robot moves its leg joints to kick a ball toward a goal. Although this is fast for a robot, people can move 20 times more quickly.

World Cup for robots

These robots are playing in RoboCup, a worldwide soccer competition for moving robots. They use sensors to know where the ball is and where their teammates are.

Robot explorers

Robots can be built to explore places that are too dangerous for people to visit. They can take pictures and send back useful information without putting people at risk.

Robo reporter

This test robot, *Afghan Explorer*, may one day visit war zones. Working as a war reporter, it could send pictures and interviews back to a TV studio in a safer place.

Into the volcano

This eight-legged robot is called *Dante II*. It can climb into the crater of a red-hot volcano to collect gas samples and take photos with its eight cameras.

Hot and cold worker

Nomad Rover is the size of a small car. It has trekked through hot deserts and icy lands all by itself, collecting information for scientists at home. In Antarctica it discovered five meteorites.

meteorite—a piece of rock or metal that has fallen to Earth from space

Underwater robots

Many robots work underwater. They map the ocean floor, monitor sea life, or find sunken shipwrecks. Robots can travel deep underwater much more easily than people can.

Unmanned submarine

Robots can stay underwater for many days at a time. They can travel hundreds of miles to explore the oceans.

monitor—to check the condition of something

Deep-sea explorer

Robots, like *Deep Drone*, can travel to the ocean floor and help recover crashed airplanes or sunken ships. *Deep Drone* can travel around 40 times deeper than unprotected human divers can.

Robot jellyfish

Some underwater robots are modeled on real sea creatures. This robot jellyfish has a small electric motor that makes it rise and fall in the water just like the real thing.

unmanned—without people onboard

Robots in space

Astronauts need special equipment in order to survive in space. Robots do not need air, water, or food. They can work on distant planets by keeping in touch with Earth using radio signals.

Photos in space

Aercam Sprint robot can zoom around the outside of a space shuttle or a space station. The beach-ball-sized robot sends images back to the astronauts inside the spacecraft.

Robot astronauts

Robonaut is a test robot built by NASA to work as a construction worker in space. It has two robot arms that can grip and use a range of tools.

Mission to Mars

NASA's *Sojourner Rover* was the first robot to travel across part of another planet. In 1997 the six-wheeled rover explored part of the surface of Mars.

NASA—*short name for the U.S. space agency*

28 Farm **robots**

Farming is hard work. Robots can help by doing some of the boring tasks that take a lot of time. Farm robots can handle small plants, help at harvesttime, or scare away pests.

Chasing birds

Scarebot is a robot that patrols catfish ponds in the United States. Its sudden movements scare away pelicans and other birds hoping to catch a fish.

programmed—giving a computer or robot a list of instructions to perform

Shear magic!

This robot from Australia has been programmed to shear the wool off a sheep. It can keep repeating the task without getting tired.

Robots at home

Robots are coming home. The latest robots are doing useful chores around the house. Home robots need to know their way around a house and be able to communicate with their owners.

Ready for breakfast?

Robots cannot cook your meals yet, but they can carry them to you. Home robots often hold a map of the house in their memory. They also need sensors to know when household objects are in their way.

communicate—to send or receive a message

Home playmates

PaPeRos wander around the house looking for people to talk to. They can recognize 650 different words and phrases and can speak up to 3,000 words. They can even dance!

Beware of the dog

This robot guard dog patrols the house, checking that everything is safe. If it notices anything wrong, it can take pictures and send them to the owner's cell phone.

Rescue robots

Some robots can save lives. They do this by fighting fires, searching for survivors after disasters, or handling dangerous objects such as unexploded bombs.

Handling bombs

Bomb disposal robots can look at suspicious packages with their cameras. They relay the information to someone at a safe distance away.

suspicious—something that may be wrong or dangerous

SEP 15 2001
11:25:01 PM

Access all areas

Packbot enters unknown areas to check for danger. In 2001 *Packbot* searched the wreckage of the World Trade Center in New York for survivors.

Fighting fires

Robots can cope with more heat than people can, and they do not need air to breathe. This makes them excellent firefighters, allowing them to get close enough to put out the flames.

At your service

Service robots are able to perform useful, repetitive, everyday tasks for people. They are willing workers and do not get bored when doing simple tasks over and over again.

Fill 'er up!

Filling your car with gas can be a tricky task—but not for this robot attendant. Its robot arm can find a car's gas tank and fill it up with the amount of gas the driver wants.

repetitive—something that is done over and over

Carry your bag

The *Intelecady* carries a bag of golf clubs around a course. The robot has a map of the course in its memory so it can avoid any bunkers or streams.

Drinks, please

Cynthia is a robot bartender at work in London, England. *Cynthia*'s robot arms can select, grip, and pour ingredients from bottles to mix customers one of 60 different drinks.

Spy robots

Human spies must be smart and sneaky. But robots can be built to get into places that humans cannot and send back information using radio signals. If spy robots are caught, they will not give away any secrets.

Mini spy
Smaller robots can travel into places without being seen. This flying robot is only six inches wide. It can fly for 30 minutes, powered by a tiny engine.

Hovering above

Cypher is a 5.9-foot-wide robot that can hover outside the windows of tall buildings. From there it can look and listen in on top secret meetings using microphones and cameras.

Watching you?

Roswell is a robot with 16 different sensors. Future spy robots may be able to identify people and follow them.

Robot doctors

Robots can work accurately for hours without making mistakes or getting tired. They make ideal assistants for human surgeons in hospital operations.

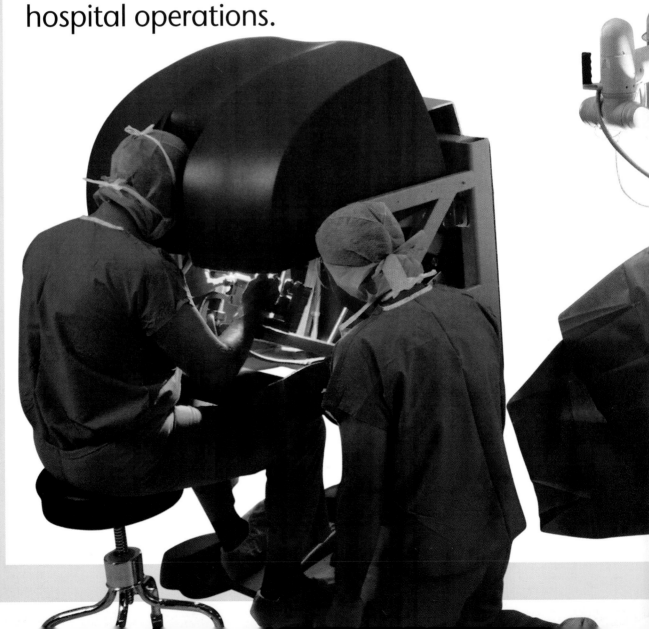

A steady hand

A human surgeon controls the *da Vinci* robot while studying a magnified view of the operation. The robot's arms are fitted with surgical tools that perform the operation.

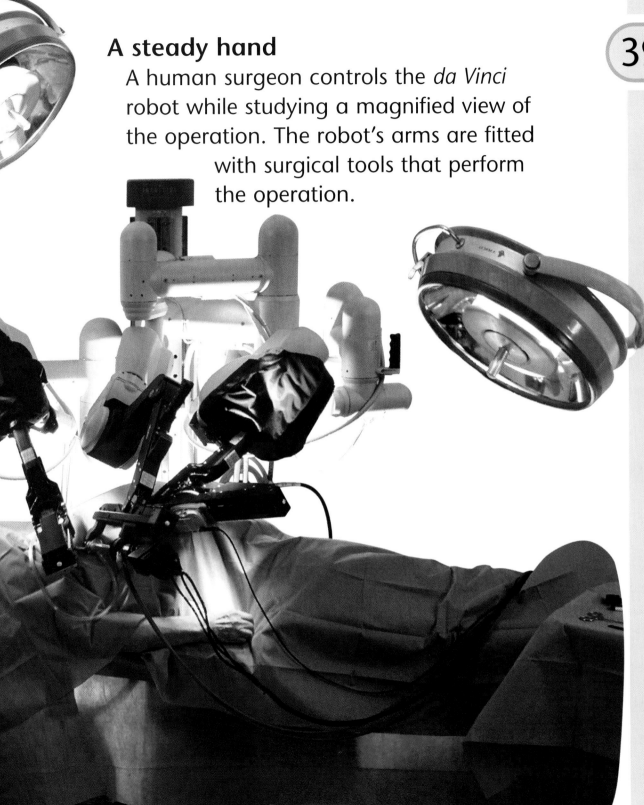

magnified—to make something look bigger

Sci-fi robots

Long before real robots were made they were popular in science-fiction books and movies. Many sci-fi robots have incredible powers and are often shown fighting to take over the world!

Short Circuit

This robot is *No.5*, the star of the movie *Short Circuit*. In the movie *No.5* was built as a robot weapon, but after being struck by lightning it refused to fight and started to learn and think for itself.

Exterminate!

Many sci-fi robots are shown as evil, including this *Dalek* from the TV show *Doctor Who*. Real robots are programmed by people, so they are only as dangerous as people make them.

Robot actors

This animatronic model of *Yoda* is from the movie *Return of the Jedi* from the *Star Wars* series. Its many electric motors allow it to make realistic movements.

42 Robot surprise!

Make a secret storage robot

Robots are very organized and find information very quickly. Make this sturdy robot storage box so that you can find your treasures whenever you need them—and keep your bedroom neat!

You will need
- Shoe box
- Small box
- Poster paints
- Paintbrush
- Scissors
- Cleaning cloth
- Glue
- Long cardboard tubes
- Candy wrappers or colored paper
- Ping-Pong™ ball
- Double-sided tape
- Pipe cleaners

1

Paint the boxes and cardboard tubes and leave them to dry. Carefully cut off the two shorter ends of the shoe box lid along the fold line.

2

Using glue or double-sided tape, attach one edge of the lid to the shoe box and press it down firmly. Cut two hand shapes from the cleaning cloth and attach a candy wrapper or colored paper to the Ping-Pong™ ball.

3

Use the smaller box for the robot's head and decorate it with pipe cleaners. Cut the long cardboard tube in half and glue one cloth hand on each. Stick these onto the sides of the box. Glue the other tubes on for feet and the wrapped ball for a handle.

44 Moving like robots

Make a moving arm

Robots can be programmed to carry out many tasks. They can pick up things and move them around. This arm can pick up paper clips.

Using the scissors, carefully cut the poster board into strips. All of the strips need to be the same length and width.

You will need

- Scissors
- 2 large sheets of poster board
- Paper fasteners and clips
- Double-sided tape or glue
- 2 small magnets

Make a crossover framework of strips and join them together with the paper fasteners. You will need to use a paper fastener in the middle of each strip, as well as at the ends.

Take two small magnets and attach them to one end of the framework. By opening and closing the other end you can use the arm to pick up paper clips.

Walk like a robot

Few robots can actually think for themselves. Most have to follow instructions. When you walk, your eyes show you where obstacles are, and your brain figures out how to avoid them. Here you can learn to move like a robot just by following instructions.

Ask a friend to help you set up a maze using furniture. Find a blindfold or close your eyes—but no peeking! Ask your friend to tell you how to walk through the maze without bumping into things. If the directions are wrong, you will hit the furniture!

46 Marvelous models

Make a model robot

Robots come in many shapes and sizes. Make a model robot using empty cartons and boxes from your home. It can be any shape or size you like.

You will need
- Boxes
- Ping-Pong™ balls
- Plastic cups
- Scissors
- Glue
- Cardboard tubes
- Tinfoil
- Ice cream carton lid
- Pipe cleaners
- Thin cardboard
- Candy wrappers or colored paper
- Tape

Using glue, carefully stick tinfoil around four cardboard tubes and a big box.

Cover another cardboard tube with colored paper and carefully cut into the ends so they will sit flat.

Glue candy wrappers or colored paper onto an ice cream carton lid and then stick it onto the big box.

Attach plastic cups to one end of the big box for the legs. Stick a piece of cardboard underneath to help it stand.

Decorate a smaller box with painted Ping-Pong™ balls and pipe cleaners. Stick the arms onto your robot.

Open out the cut ends of the decorated cardboard tube and attach it to the head and body.

Index